Funding and Financing For Programs To Serve K–3 At-Risk Children

The Authors

K. Forbis Jordan is Professor of Educational Leadership and Policy Studies, College of Education, Arizona State University, Tempe.

Teresa S. Lyons is Assistant Professor of Educational Administration and Supervision, University of Nevada at Las Vegas.

John T. McDonough is an Administrative Assistant, Romeo Public Schools, Michigan.

Funding and Financing for Programs to Serve K–3 At-Risk Children:

A Research Review

K. Forbis Jordan, Teresa S. Lyons, and
John T. McDonough

Reference & Resource Series

nea PROFESSIONAL LIBRARY
National Education Association
Washington, D.C.

Printing History
    First Printing: January 1992

Note

The opinions expressed in this publication should not be construed as representing the policy or position of the National Education Association. Materials published by the NEA Professional Library are intended to be discussion documents for teachers who are concerned with specialized interests of the profession.

Library of Congress Cataloging-in-Publication Data

Jordan, K. Forbis (Kenneth Forbis), 1930–
    Funding and financing for programs to serve K-3 at-risk children:
a research review/K. Forbis Jordan, Teresa S. Lyons, John T.
McDonough.
        p.   cm.—(Reference & resource series)
    "NEA professional library."
    Includes bibliographical references (p.   ).
    ISBN 0-8106-1542-8
    1. Socially handicapped children—Education—United States—
Finance. 2. State aid to education—United States.   I. Lyons,
Teresa S.   II. McDonough, John T.   III. Title.   IV. Series.
LC4091.J636   1992
379.1'222—dc20   91–19436
                                                                CIP

CONTENTS

Chapter 1

FUNDING AND FINANCING PROGRAMS FOR K–3 AT-RISK CHILDREN: AN INTRODUCTION

WHY HAS THE CONCERN DEVELOPED?

The importance of improving educational opportunities for primary age children has become a matter of national concern. The need for quality education experiences for primary age children has been reinforced by the current educational reform movement; over two dozen national reform reports have been presented since the publication of *A Nation At Risk* in 1983. The reform movement has focused on the following three broad concerns (Committee for Economic Development 1987):

- Raising standards and expectations for students
- Improving the quality of the teaching profession
- Meeting the needs of at-risk youth

Recently, an interest in primary-age at-risk children has been shown in the educational goals adopted by President Bush and the National Governors' Association (1990). Their first goal refers to children being "ready" to enter school; that is one of the driving interests behind programs for disadvantaged preschool and primary grade children. The goal is to reduce the long-term social and economic impact of having large numbers of minimally educated youth who do not possess the level of skills required to be effective in the work force. Early intervention is considered to be an essential component of the reform interest in raising standards and expectations for students.

The national interest in intervention programs for at-risk youth in the 1990s is not a new concern, but can be traced to the enactment of Title I programs for the educationally disadvantaged through the Elementary and Secondary Education Act and the Federal Head Start program. From the results of an analysis of 65 research studies, Lennon (1989) concluded that, for primary grade children, linkages can be found between lower socioeconomic conditions and low school performance and that the probability of low performance increases when the number of factors is greater.

COST TO SOCIETY OF NONINTERVENTION

Educational economists have argued in favor of funding at-risk programs because of the cost to society if the present situation is allowed to continue. Levin (1989) asserted that the social benefits of investing in at-risk programming are likely to be well in excess of the costs of providing such programs. He projected that a serious effort would require an additional annual expenditure nationally in excess of $25 billion. However, the cost of the current dropout problem on the national level reflects $71 billion in lost tax revenues, $3 billion in increased welfare and unemployment costs, and $3 billion in crime-related costs (Grossnickle 1986; Hodgkinson 1985; Kunisawa 1988; Natriello, Pallas, and McDill 1987). Such high social and economic costs suggest that it would be cost effective to invest in early intervention programs for students who are potentially at risk of dropping out of the educational system.

Early intervention may appear costly, but Owen Butler, the retired chairman of Procter and Gamble, has contended that the investment is sound when considered in terms of the social and economic cost of neglect and is small when compared to the total public school expenditures. Each year's class of dropouts costs the nation more than $240 billion in lost earnings and foregone taxes in their lifetime. A relatively economical way to address this problem would be to provide full funding of Head Start at an annual cost of about $12 billion, less than 10 percent of the total expenditures on K–12 education (Butler 1989). Brown (1985) also has noted that early intervention results in a reduction of the number of students assigned to special education, a reduction in the number of students retained, increases in achievement in the early primary years, and higher self-esteem.

POLICY CONFLICT

The critical question is how the demand for preschool and primary early intervention programs can be balanced against the urgent need for educational services for older at-risk students (Hebbeler 1985; Slavin, Karweit, and Madden 1989). Edelman (1989) also noted this policy conflict, but stressed the need to address the educational needs of younger disadvantaged children because "today's child is tomorrow's worker." She emphasized that the nation cannot afford to waste the resource of its youth if America is to compete in the world market. Edelman contended that the early investment in child care and educational interventions is vital to the continued economic health of the nation.

Chapter 2

IMPORTANT QUESTIONS

WHO IS AT RISK?

Precise and uniformly accepted definitions for at-risk students have not been developed. However, various reports have identified characteristics or indicators of at-risk students that school districts have utilized to target students who need additional help. These indicators represent a complex set of personal, socioeconomic, and school characteristics that have a significant impact on children's success in matriculating through the educational system. A synthesis of recent literature and research on at-risk students reveals that they have one or more of the following characteristics (Brodinsky 1989; Davis and McCaul 1990; Fine 1987; Hahn, Danzberger, and Lefkowitz 1987; Mann 1987; Ralph 1989; Wehlage and Rutter 1986):

1. Are from a home in which the income is below the poverty level
2. Are chemically dependent
3. Have a poor attendance record
4. Demonstrate a dislike for school
5. Show poor academic performance relative to the student body
6. Receive poor grades
7. Have undiagnosed learning disabilities or emotional problems, and
8. Are older than their peers.

Rather than looking at the characteristics of individual students (as illustrated in the above synthesis), some researchers have looked at the entire school population for indications of being at risk. Schools with large at-risk populations are identified by high percentages of the following (Brodinsky 1989; Hahn, Danzberger, and Lefkowitz 1987; Mann 1987; Natriello, Pallas, and McDill 1987; Orr 1987; Ralph 1989; Wehlage and Rutter 1986):

1. students who come from low-income homes;
2. students whose academic performance, behavior, and attendance can be characterized as poor;
3. students retained in one or more grades;
4. student mobility; and
5. student feelings of alienation.

Additionally, states have developed at-risk profiles to project characteristics of future school populations and to identify key factors in the state that may

Table 1
Arizona At-Risk Profile

Poverty (1988):	Estimated 13% of the population (475,000 people)
Free and reduced lunch (1988-89):	Over 29% (188,808) of Arizona's K-12 students
Minority students (1987):	35.5% of elementary school students
Limited English proficient (1987-88):	7.2% (44,676) of K-12 students; 41.5% increase since FY 1984-85
Iowa Test of Basic Skills (1986-87):	19% of K-3 students below the 25th percentile; 42% of 7-12 students below the 40th percentile
Graduation rate (1987):	64.4%, while national average was 71.1%
Arizona cost for high school dropouts (1987):	Estimated at $5.39 billion annually
Penal Institution Inmates (1987):	85%-90% are high school dropouts
Divorce rate (1987):	Third highest among 48 reporting states
Single-parent households (1989):	Estimated 27% of all households
Births to unwed mothers (1987):	27% of Arizona births (17,000)—nearly twice the 1975 rate
Teen pregnancy (1986):	9th highest in the nation; on average, 32 teens become pregnant each day
Drug usage (1988):	Of 9th grade students, 27% have tried marijuana, 9% cocaine, 20% inhalants
Suicide rate (1987):	20.9 per 100,000 among teenagers age 15-19; 39% increase over previous year
Juvenile arrests (1987):	20.8% of total arrests; 11.8% (5,435) of these were age 12 or under
Public assistance benefit level (1987):	Ranked 37th in nation
Mental health funding per capita (1987):	Ranked last in nation

Source: *1988-89 Status and Evaluation Report: The Arizona At-Risk Pilot Project: Serving Students in Grades K-3 and 7-12 Pursuant of HB 2217,* p. 15 Morrison Institute for Public Policy, Tempe, Ariz.: School of Public Affairs, Arizona State University, November 1989.

contribute to the at-risk issue. (See Table 1 for the key factors used in Arizona.) While it is not expected that schools alone can solve all of the aforementioned problems, educators can use the descriptive research to recognize at-risk conditions that affect children's lives and determine appropriate programs to meet those identified needs within the context of the educational setting.

WHAT DEFINITIONS DO STATES USE?

Historically, much of the funding for programs to serve these children can be attributed to their being classified as "handicapped" or "disadvantaged." Such students could participate in special education programs and programs for the educationally disadvantaged. Federal funding has been provided for both programs, state funding has been provided for special education, and a few states provide state funds for special programs for educationally disadvantaged

Table 2
State Definitions of At-Risk Youth

ARIZONA	At-risk youth are defined as those students who have dropped out or who have identifiable characteristics, including academic and economic factors, which are recognized as increasing the likelihood of their dropping out of the educational system.
CALIFORNIA	At-risk students may be described as pupils who are victims of extenuating circumstance and/or are exhibiting behaviors that result in participation in gang activities. These circumstances and behaviors may include child abuse, poverty, inadequate housing, inadequate nutrition, delinquency, absenteeism, and alcohol and drug abuse.
GEORGIA	The state definition defines at-risk children at three educational levels: preschool, primary grades, and intermediate-secondary grades. Among the characteristics cited that place a child at risk are: living in poverty, limited English proficiency, poor academic performance, retention in one or more grades, frequent absences, emotional problems, health problems, behavior problems, student's use of alcohol or drugs, pregnancy or parenthood, and attempted suicide.

(continued on next page)

11

Table 2   *(continued)*

IOWA

A student is at risk who is in danger of not meeting the goals of the educational program established by the district, not completing a high school education, or not becoming a productive worker. These students may include, but are not limited to, dropouts, potential dropouts, teenage parents, substance users and abusers, low academic achievers, abused and homeless children, youth offenders, economically deprived, minority students, and culturally isolated; those with sudden negative changes in performance due to environmental or physical trauma; and those with language barriers, gender barriers, and disabilities.

KANSAS

At risk pupil means any person of school age who is at risk of failing at or dropping out of school and who may be characterized by one or more of the following: (1) has an excessive rate of unexcused absences from school attendance; (2) is a parent or is pregnant and will become a parent; (3) has been adjudicated as a juvenile offender; (4) is two or more credits behind other pupils in the same age group in the number of graduation credits attained; or (5) has been retained one or more grades. The definition of at-risk pupil shall not include within its meaning any person determined to be an exceptional child under the provisions of the Special Education for Exceptional Children Act.

NORTH CAROLINA

Children and youth at risk in North Carolina are young people, who because of a wide range of personal, familial, social, or academic circumstances, may experience school failure or unwanted outcomes unless there is intervention to reduce the risk factors. Primary factors that may identify these children include the following: school performance at two or more years below grade level; CAT scores below the 25th percentile; academic failure; nonpromotion (being older than classmates); truancy; substance abuse; delinquency; disinterest in school; low self-esteem; learning disabilities; physical, mental, or emotional handicaps; physical or mental health problems; physical or sexual abuse; pregnancy; unstable

(continued on next page)

Table 2 *(continued)*

home environmental/family trauma; family income at or below the poverty level; negative parental attitudes toward school; low parental educational attainment; frustration of unchallenged giftedness and unrecognized talent; and limited English proficiency.

OKLAHOMA

At-risk youth are members of a household or family whose income is at or below the poverty level under criteria used by the U.S. Bureau of the Census; or they have not made substantial progress in mastering skills that are appropriate for students of their age; or they have grades that consistently indicate major underachievement; or they have been retained in a grade for one or more years; or they have been a school dropout or have had excessive absences during a school year; or they have been determined to be at risk based on assessment by school staff familiar with the students' health, social, or family status. Influences may include, but are not limited to, evidence of abuse of the students, the students' use of alcohol or drugs, pregnancy or parenthood, delinquent behavior, or attempted suicide.

PENNSYLVANIA

The term "student at risk" at the most general level refers to any elementary or secondary student who runs the risk of not acquiring the knowledge, skills, and attitudes needed to become a successful adult. More specifically, at risk refers to students who behave in ways that put them at risk of not graduating from high school. These behaviors include not engaging in classroom and school activities, using drugs and alcohol, committing disruptive and delinquent acts, becoming pregnant, dropping out, or attempting suicide—behaviors that would not be expected of students who, in particular, had acquired the knowledge, skills, and citizenship, family living, health, and work. Finally, the term refers to students whose family background and home and community conditions (e.g., poverty, low parental education) correlate with low achievement and the lack of school success.

students. More recently states have targeted monies specifically for at-risk students. In a survey conducted by McDonough (1990), 17 of 50 states reported that they provide some funding, primarily through competitive discretionary grants and categorical funding, for programs to serve at-risk students.

In a recent survey of states, McDonough (1990) investigated the methods currently used in each state to define the target population of at-risk youth. He found that 29 states had no official definition of at-risk youth. Limited definitions focusing on factors relative to student academic performance were found in 15 states. In 8 states, comprehensive definitions enumerated both academic and socioeconomic factors contributing to a student's being at risk of not completing school. McDonough found a wide range of definitions, confirming the fact that there is no uniformly accepted definition of at-risk youth. (See Table 2 for a list of the eight states with comprehensive definitions.)

WHAT KINDS OF PROGRAMS SHOULD BE PROVIDED?

Educational programming for at-risk youth has become increasingly important as a topic of high interest in public-policy discussions. Earlier, the prevailing attitude often was that a significant number of youth could be expected to become disaffected with school and could fill a set of menial jobs in the labor market. The willingness to accept an attitude of benign neglect about these youth became less tolerable because of changes in the patterns of the American family structure, structural employment shifts in the job market, and social problems related to drugs and chemical dependency. In the 1980s, national concerns about the declining performance of American students and the need for the nation to become more competitive in the world economy resulted in greater public attention being given to the performance of all students, not just those who "want to learn." The developing consensus was that many of these youth had special educational needs, that they needed special programs, and that funding for programs to serve these youth should, at least in part, be provided by state governments.

Conceptual discussions related to "desirable approaches" to be used in providing state funds for programs to serve at-risk youth have evolved in a manner different from the ways in which need-based funding approaches were developed for special education programs. Rather than relying on a research base, funding approaches for special education often were conceptualized in the abstract by members of the intellectual community and then placed in state regulations imposed on local school districts. The passage of P.L. 94–142 and the resulting federal regulations contributed to the acceptance of a series of untested assumptions about the best way to provide special education services. Under this scenario, little opportunity was provided for local flexibility, ingenuity, or initiative.

A different history is evolving relative to programs to serve at-risk youth. Persons seeking to initiate programs to serve at-risk youth have access to an intellectual base similar to that which existed relative to special education, but schools are exploring a variety of approaches in the absence of detailed regulations about programs and in an effort to accelerate the pace of program development. The pattern of program evolution is that local schools identify priorities and organize program delivery systems in response to their locally perceived needs and available funds. Different approaches have been initiated and are evolving as a result of success and failure experiences, local management constraints, staff and community interest, and available funds. This has resulted in a plethora of programs that are often unique and innovative and that have, in some cases, resulted in the reassessment and restructuring of the total educational setting to better meet the needs of all students.

In a survey of the states, Coley and Goertz (1987) identified four elements of effective strategies for meeting the needs of at-risk youth:

1. Collaboration and coordination
2. Staff and parental involvement in program planning and implementation
3. Emphasis on prevention and early intervention
4. Opportunities for nontraditional education experiences

Chapter 3

FOCUS ON THE RESEARCH

WHAT DOES THE RESEARCH SAY?

Considerable research has been conducted on Head Start programs for preschool children. The studies have found that attitudes toward school were more positive, and early intervention programs benefited the entire family. Children who participated showed positive gains over those who did not participate (Goldring and Presbrey 1986). However, questions remain as to the extent to which consistent and long-term academic achievement gains can be maintained and the degree to which early intervention efforts will enable disadvantaged students to compete on an equal footing with other students.

Research is limited on the relative effectiveness of specific instructional approaches that might be used in teaching low-income, primary-age youth. Gersten, Darch, and Gleason (1988) compared the performance at the third and ninth grades of students who received the direct instruction approach in kindergarten with those who did not receive an academic instructional approach in kindergarten. Results for students at the end of both the third and ninth grades supported the academic instructional approach in kindergarten. To gain a better understanding of the progress, Gersten recommended process-product naturalistic studies to isolate and clarify the instructional variables and student interactions linked to growth in student learning and self-concept. Rather than having an immediate immersion in academics, Gersten reported that the focus in kindergarten was on a gradual and systematic transition between the child-centered kindergarten and the structured environment of most first grades. The goals were to build the skills and knowledge necessary for success in first grade and to help students increase their attention span and ability to focus on academic material. Gersten emphasized that one of the critical considerations in this type of program was the clear and direct alignment between the skills taught in kindergarten and the content of the first grade curriculum.

The interaction between social competence and academic survival skills has been viewed as critical to a child's success in kindergarten and the primary grades (Foulks and Morrow 1989). However, they also noted the existence of minimal research related to academic survival skills and social competence in kindergarten. Especially for the at-risk child, the goal is to become independent, self-sufficient, and socially competent. Foulks and Morrow stated that systematic research was limited on the specific skills needed by young children at risk of school failure. Lyons (1990b) in a study of at-risk kindergartners, found that low language skills were the consistent identifier for children placed in developmental, or extra year, kindergarten programs. In a study of programs in a three-county area in northern California, they found that the two most critical skills for a child's successful adjustment to kindergarten were that the child listens carefully to teacher instructions and directions and that the child complies with teacher demands.

The focus on academics has been challenged by different researchers (Shepherd and Smith 1986; Charlesworth 1989). The concern is that the curriculum in the upper grades is being pushed to lower levels, and large numbers of students are doomed to failure. This counterposition is that kindergarten should serve a readiness function that prepares children for schooling, rather than an experience for which students need to be prepared when they arrive. The issue then becomes whether the child should be ready for the school or the school should be ready for the child. The alternative movement is toward a developmental placement system that involves a continuous progress plan with multi-age grouping. This is reflected in the recent school reform legislation in Kentucky that has mandated an ungraded K–3 program. Even though the debate over the best approach may continue, there seems to be agreement that the program needs to fit the child's pre-operational learning style. If a school adopts the child-centered, developmentally appropriate approach that matches learning experiences to children, the implication is that serious consideration will be given to continuous progress and multi-age grouping. Charlesworth (1989) contended that success will be dependent on the degree to which the teacher and parents are involved in planning and decision making from the outset so that they have a sense of ownership and understand the program.

In a review of model programs for at-risk youth, Peck, Law, and Mills (1987) drew several general conclusions regarding the core elements of successful programs. Programs should be student centered; families should be involved; and special attention should be given to staff selection and training. They also found that successful programs had organizational and administrative arrangements to assist teachers.

Although empirical research is limited on what works for at-risk youth, the body of data is increasing. Two studies conducted at Johns Hopkins University (Slavin and Madden 1987; Madden and Slavin 1987) examined effective classroom and pull-out programs for students at risk. Program in these studies was defined as "a set of procedures intended to be implemented as a total package and capable of being replicated by others" (Slavin and Madden 1987,i). The programs had as their focus increased achievement in reading and/or math in grades one through six.

CATEGORIES OF EFFECTIVE PROGRAMS

Effective classroom programs fell into three major categories: continuous progress, cooperative learning, and individualized instruction. Effective pull-out programs also fell into three major categories: tutoring, computer-assisted instruction (CAI), and diagnostic-prescriptive activities. Results of Slavin and Madden's (1987) research revealed that:

> the most consistently successful classroom models were continuous progress programs in which students are taught in skill-level groups and proceed through a hierarchical set of skills, and cooperative learning programs in which students also receive instruction at their appropriate levels, but then practice skills in mixed-ability learning teams. (p.15)

On the basis of this and other evidence, they concluded that "effective programs for students at-risk balance adjustment of instructional approaches to meet students' unique needs with provision of adequate direct instruction. In addition, effective classroom programs provide frequent assessment of student progress through a well-specified, hierarchical set of skills" (p. 15). The examination of effective pull-out programs supported these same conclusions (Madden and Slavin 1987): "the most successful models, tutoring and CAI, completely adapt instruction to students' unique needs and provide plentiful direct instruction appropriate to students' levels of readiness"(p. 16).

Slavin and Madden (1987) concluded that an increase in student achievement can be accomplished either by making relatively inexpensive but extensive modifications in the regular instructional program (such as continuous progress programs), or by implementing relatively expensive but intensive pull-out programs (such as one-on-one tutoring and CAI). The authors suggested that a combination of these strategies may be more effective than either one by itself.

Chapter 4

CLASSIFICATION AND ANALYSIS
OF AT-RISK PROGRAMMING

PROGRAM OPTIONS

The National Association for the Education of Young Children and the National Governors' Association have identified the central elements of high-quality early childhood programs. They include competent and qualified teachers, a developmental curriculum, sensitivity to cultural diversity and minority children and their families, a low child-staff ratio, involvement of child-care specialists and early childhood professionals, and active involvement and participation of parents (Curry 1990).

In the design of programs, a series of questions merit the attention of policymakers (Schweinhart and Weikart 1986). The ones with direct reference to K–3 programs are whether programs should be available to all children, whether the program should be full-day or half-day, whether the program should be free or on an ability to pay basis, and whether the program should be compulsory or voluntary. The latter issue is critical if demonstrated scholastic readiness is a condition for entry into first grade.

The period of time that the program will operate will be influenced by the degree to which consideration is to be given to the parents' workday. If the program is to include child care, the length of the child's stay will be longer, and the program will extend through normal school vacations. If the choice is a full-day program, attention must be given to the overall quality of the program and the potential fatigue and behavioral issues associated with young children.

TYPES OF CURRENT AT-RISK PROGRAMS

Because of the wide variety of at-risk programs that currently exist, several researchers have suggested that a conceptual framework or classification model should be developed to identify the essential elements in current programs (Cox 1985; Clifford 1987; Roberts 1990).

Classification Systems

Early efforts to classify at-risk programs had two primary approaches (Clifford 1987). The first approach looked at program components related to elements such as size of the program, community linkages, student-teacher ratio, and resource materials. The second approach to classifying programs looked at program focus. Examples of program focus components included counseling, basic skills remediation, vocational training and awareness, and social support services.

A classification of programs based upon program focus was also reported by Cox (1985), who examined dropout prevention programs in Appalachian school districts. He classified programs using seven focus clusters:

1. Tutorial activities
2. Alternative curriculum or classes
3. Work-related activities
4. Counseling/advising
5. Attitudinal/self-awareness activities
6. Attendance incentives
7. Parental involvement

Clifford (1987) synthesized the two approaches for classifying programs and tested his taxonomy on 25 dropout-prevention programs. His classification procedures resulted in a content analysis of at-risk programs based on a curriculum framework. Variables in Clifford's taxonomy included data about objectives, learner diagnosis, program content, program delivery, resources, and pupil progress.

Roberts (1990) adapted and expanded Clifford's classification system for analyzing at-risk programs. She categorized 200 at-risk programs in 15 school districts using a three-dimensional model. Roberts looked at all levels of programming including K–3 programs for at-risk children. The program variables in her model were focus, strategy, and delivery. Each of the three primary program variables had subcomponents. Program focus categorized the primary emphasis of programs into four areas: academic, vocational, soci-oemotional, and parent/family. Program strategies grouped intervention approaches into three types: integrated programs within the regular classroom, nonintegrated resource-based programs, and alternative programs conducted off-campus. The program delivery dimension identified the primary means of delivering services: one-to-one, small group, and classroom. (see Figure 1).

The results of Roberts' (1990) classification study showed that the three most commonly occurring types of programs accounted for 41.5 percent of the 200 programs studied. The most frequently occurring programs were categorized in the academic non-integrated class cluster. Of these programs, 22 were special classes providing basic skills remediation. Of the 15 selected districts in her study, 12 had programs of this type. Programs in the academic nonintegrated small group cluster were the second most frequent type of program. The majority of these programs were resource pull-out programs, such as ESL instruction, tutoring, reading assistance, and math assistance. Nine of the 15 selected districts had programs of this type. Programs in the academic

Figure 1
A Classification Model for At-Risk Programs

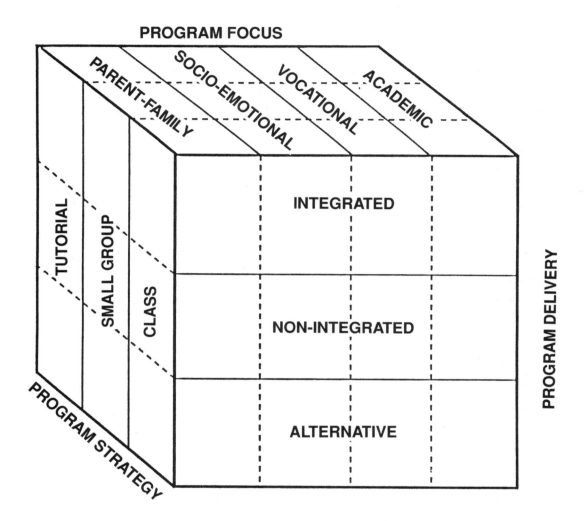

Source: "Classification and Analysis of Delivery Systems for At-Risk Programs in Selected School Districts," by C. D. Roberts (Arizona State University, Tempe). © C. D. Roberts, 1990. Reprinted with permission.

integrated class cluster were the third most common type of program. The majority of these programs were early prevention efforts, such as extended day kindergarten and K–3 academic assistance within the regular classroom setting. Nine districts had this type of program.

Roberts (1990) found that these three program clusters, and an additional five program clusters focusing on counseling/social services and tutoring assistance, accounted for 79.5 percent of the programs offered in the sampled districts. These findings were consistent with a GAO report (1987) that stated that services for at-risk youth usually involved academic basic skills instruction, counseling, and social service assistance.

Lyons (1990a) in a follow-up of the Roberts study examined 100 additional at-risk programs funded through state-awarded discretionary grants in Arizona. When the distribution of programs was compared according to Roberts' classification model, the findings were similar except in two areas. There were no schoolwide/ classroom-based prevention programs such as "Just Say No" and "Good Touch, Bad Touch." These are typically low-cost programs and may be funded through federal grants, so districts had no incentive to apply for state funding. The second area of difference was in the increase of integrated classroom-based programs in the discretionary grants sample. There are two possible explanations for this. First, the state grant requested documentation of how the services would be integrated; this resulted in a strong incentive for school districts to design a program with integrated services to increase the probability that the proposal would be funded. Second, the programs in the discretionary grant sample were newer programs; their design likely benefited from updated information in the research literature that supported the contention that integrated services, as opposed to pull-out programs, may be optimal for at-risk students.

In a national survey administered through the Council of Chief State School Officers, Coley and Goertz (1987) identified a small number of state programs at the preschool and elementary levels. Among those states providing early intervention programs were Louisiana, Maryland, and Oregon. Louisiana was operating a program for four-year-olds that was developmental and based on child-initiated activities. Students were selected from the Head Start waiting lists, siblings of Chapter 1 students, children from low-income families, and siblings of former program participants. Those students with the greatest developmental lags were selected for the program.

Maryland's program was for four-year-olds in at-risk schools, i.e., schools with average third grade reading comprehension scores at least six months below national norms. The program focused on language and concept development and includes cross-grade communication and home-school cooperation activities (Coley and Goertz 1987).

Oregon provided a child development specialist program that places emphasis on K–3 programs. This program focused on developmental student needs and emphasizes development of a positive self-concept, skills in human relations, and acceptance of responsibility as a prerequisite for academic learning (Coley and Goertz 1987).

Coley and Goertz (1987) also described several programs operated by local school districts. Montclair (N.J.) was identifying and providing services to at-risk preschool and kindergarten children who exhibit difficulties in cognitive or linguistic development. Columbus (Ohio) had a one-on-one intervention program for the poorest readers in first grade classrooms. Williamsburg (Va.) was operating a collaborative program with another agency for children from birth through five years. Classroom instruction, home visits, and sharing centers were being provided with an emphasis in parental involvement.

The variety of programming being developed by school districts was evidenced in an evaluation study of at-risk programs in Arizona conducted by the Morrison Institute (1989). The Institute found several key intervention strategies for K–3 at-risk programs (see Table 3). The strategies involved six primary areas: modification in curriculum and instruction, extended school services, parent involvement, staff development, staff additions, and support services.

WHY SHOULD PROGRAMS BE FUNDED?

As a result of the relatively recent recognition that special programs funds should be provided for at-risk children, securing adequate funds for these programs is a continuing challenge. If sufficient programs and services are to be provided for at-risk students, the state—which has the primary responsibility for ensuring that children have access to an adequate education—has a special interest in identifying program costs and methods for allocating state funds to support programs and activities for at-risk students. A general principle in school finance is that the cost of an educational program is influenced by the varying characteristics of students and school districts. Thus, "providing the same resources for all students and all school districts will not ensure that educational programs are adequate and equitable" (Webb, McCarthy, and Thomas 1988, 148).

While the initial thrust of school finance reform was horizontal equity (i.e., the equal treatment of equals), more recently attention has been given to the concept of vertical equity (i.e., unequal treatment of unequals) (Webb, McCarthy, and Thomas 1988). Chambers (1981) stated that "vertical student educational equity or more simply educational equity may be said to be attained when the quantity and mix of school resources and services vary in direct relation to discernible differences in the educational needs of students" (p. 5).

The rationale for the unequal allocation of resources based on educational need rests on the social justice principle. The contention of the social justice principle is that:

> neither children nor school systems operate in isolation from society, but function within the larger social system which, absent government subventions, tends to produce resource flows that correlate with factors such as social status and wealth. (Hodge 1981, 7)

The allocation of supplemental resources to populations with special needs such as at-risk youth thus becomes a defensible position in light of the social justice principle:

> While the educational system is unable to compensate fully for social and economic imbalances, it is generally recognized to be one of the prime vehicles of upward mobility. The attempt to overcome systematic disadvantages has therefore been viewed as an important role of education. (Hodge 1981, 9).

An implicit assumption in the social justice principle is that efforts to compensate school systems for different levels of spending potentially increase the benefits of education and strengthen society in general (Hansen 1980). Both Levin (1989) and Sherman (1987) have advocated the allocation of specific funds to meet the needs of at-risk students. From an economic viewpoint, Levin (1989) argued in favor of funding at-risk programs because of the cost to society if the present situation is allowed to continue. He contended that those costs include (1) the creation of a dual-class society, (2) disruption of higher education, (3) reduced national and state economic competitiveness, and (4) higher public service costs associated with poverty and crime. The high social and economic costs of "no action" suggest that it would be cost effective to invest in programs for students at-risk of dropping out of the educational system. Such an effort, Levin maintained, would be best accomplished by the coordinated efforts of federal, state, and local governmental units to increase funding efforts for at-risk programs.

Intervention Strategies K-3 At-Risk Programs

CURRICULUM & INSTRUCTION:

School	ESL Program Enrichment	Expanded Library Resources/Bookmobile	Classroom Library	Content Area Resource Centers	Written Individual Education Plan	Computer Assisted Instruction	Non-graded Primary Classes	Same Teacher over Multiple Years	Integrated Classroom Activities/Field Trips	Curriculum Integration Using Thematic Units	Literacy Based/Whole Language Approach	"Hands On" Math (Manipulatives)	Awards/Incentives	Magnet At Risk Classroom(s)	Academic Tutoring
Ash Fork		●		●					●	●	●	●	●		
Chinle		●	●	●		●	●		●	●	●		●		●
Coolidge		●						●	●	●	●	●			●
Creighton			●	●					●	●	●	●			●
Ganado	●	●	●	●	●	●	●		●	●	●	●	●		●
Kayenta		●	●				●	●	●	●	●	●			●
Laveen				●	●				●	●	●				
Littleton				●					●	●	●	●			●
Mary C. O'Brien	●			●		●			●	●	●				●
Morristown			●						●	●			●		●
Murphy			●	●		●			●	●	●				
Nogales	●					●									●
Osborn			●			●			●	●	●				●
Page		●	●	●	●	●					●	●	●		●
Phoenix Elementary			●						●	●		●			
Picacho	●	●	●		●	●			●	●	●	●	●		●
Roosevelt	●	●	●	●	●				●	●	●	●	●	●	●
San Carlos	●		●						●	●	●	●	●		●
Sanders	●	●	●	●		●	●	●	●	●	●		●		●
Somerton	●	●								●	●				●
Whiteriver	●		●			●			●	●		●			●
Wilson	●			●		●				●	●	●			

Table 3 (continued)

Intervention Strategies K-3 At-Risk Programs

Intervention Strategies	Ash Fork	Chinle	Coolidge	Creighton	Ganado	Kayenta	Laveen	Littleton	Mary C. O'Brien	Morristown	Murphy	Nogales	Osborn	Page	Phoenix Elementary	Picacho	Roosevelt	San Carlos	Sanders	Somerton	Whiteriver	Wilson
EXTENDED SCHOOL SERVICES:																						
After-School Program	•				•					•		•	•	•		•	•			•	•	
Extended Summer Program and Services	•	•	•	•	•	•			•		•	•	•	•	•	•	•	•	•	•		
All-Day or Extended Kindergarten			•				•	•	•		•				•		•					•
PARENT INVOLVEMENT:																						
Written Contract	•				•											•			•			
Regularly Scheduled Phone Call/Written Report	•	•	•	•	•			•	•	•		•	•	•		•	•		•			•
Regularly Scheduled Newsletter			•			•	•	•		•		•	•				•	•		•	•	•
Home Visits	•	•	•	•	•	•	•	•	•	•	•		•	•		•	•	•	•	•	•	•
Home-Based Instruction	•	•					•										•	•	•			•
Parent Training Classes	•	•	•	•	•		•	•	•		•	•	•	•	•	•	•	•	•	•	•	•
Adult Education Classes		•		•			•	•	•					•		•			•			•
Parents on K-3 Advisory Committee	•		•	•	•			•			•			•		•	•	•			•	•
School Volunteer Program		•	•						•	•		•		•		•	•	•	•			•

Table 3 (continued)

Intervention Strategies K-3 At-Risk Programs

	Ash Fork	Chinle	Coolidge	Creighton	Ganado	Kayenta	Laveen	Littleton	Mary C. O'Brien	Morristown	Murphy	Nogales	Osborn	Page	Phoenix Elementary	Picacho	Roosevelt	San Carlos	Sanders	Somerton	Whiteriver	Wilson
STAFF DEVELOPMENT:																						
Weekly				•							•							•	•	•	•	
Monthly						•	•	•			•				•		•					•
Occasionally during Semester		•	•		•		•	•	•	•		•	•									
Summer Training	•		•	•			•	•		•			•						•			•
STAFF ADDITIONS:																						
Instructional Aide		•		•	•				•	•		•	•		•	•	•	•	•	•	•	•
Classroom Teacher		•	•	•	•		•	•	•	•	•				•		•	•				•
Resource Teacher		•												•								
Project Director/Coordinator			•	•		•						•						•	•	•		
Parent Liaison/Outreach Worker		•	•	•				•	•		•	•		•		•	•			•	•	
Counselor		•						•														
Classified Staff			•	•	•											•	•	•				
Other					•		•	•						•							•	

Table 3 (continued)

Intervention Strategies K-3 At-Risk Programs

SERVICES:	Ash Fork	Chinle	Coolidge	Creighton	Ganado	Kayenta	Laveen	Littleton	Mary C. O'Brien	Morristown	Murphy	Nogales	Osborn	Page	Phoenix Elementary	Picacho	Roosevelt	San Carlos	Sanders	Somerton	Whiteriver	Wilson
Counseling	●	●					●	●						●				●				
Transportation (Students and/or Parents)	●	●							●	●		●	●			●	●					
Child Care for Families	●	●	●	●					●				●			●						●
Recreational Activities		●								●						●						

Source: 1988–89 Status and Evaluation Report: The Arizona At-Risk Pilot Project: Serving Students in Grades K–3 and 7–12 Pursuant of HB 2217. Morrison Institute for Public Policy. Tempe, Ariz.: School of Public Affairs, Arizona State University, November 1989.

Chapter 5

STATE FUNDING OF AT-RISK PROGRAMS

HOW ARE THE STATES FUNDING PROGRAMS FOR AT-RISK YOUTH?

During the last several years, state policymakers have responded to the problem by allocating funds specifically targeted at dropout prevention and at programs to serve at-risk youth. Several states' efforts, including California, Florida, New York, and North Carolina, have been funded at relatively high levels and have been well documented (Sherman 1987). A recent survey of state agencies (McDonough 1990) found that 17 of the 50 states had some allocation of funds targeted to at-risk youth. Selected programs, such as teen parent and drug prevention programs, were funded in 22 states (see Table 4).

States are currently using a variety of mechanisms to fund at-risk programs, but the most common types are competitive discretionary grants and categorical funding. While some have criticized the discretionary grant approach, which has been used to fund demonstration grants and grants for research and dissemination, others have suggested that, given the current "state of the art," this strategy is a legitimate response to the problem:

> Since the research literature does not provide any definitive answers about "what works" in dropout prevention, and since resources are relatively scarce, experimentation with different program models is an appropriate way to deal with the dropout problem before large-scale funding is undertaken. (Sherman 1987, 34)

Currently, most funds are distributed by the state, based on budgeted or anticipated costs. Districts submit budgets with grant proposals based on the anticipated costs for delivering services. Thus, funding to date for at-risk programs is based primarily on grants to cover total program costs rather than on unit costs such as per-pupil costs (Sherman 1987). Before other types of funding strategies can be considered (for example, categorical grants per pupil or pupil weights), cost information in unit cost terms must be available.

A key factor influencing the cost of at-risk programs is the type of services to be provided. As Levin (1989) stated, there is a wide range of costs involved in providing services for at-risk students. Sherman (1987) remarked that "ideally, research would be available to policy-makers that provides definitive answers about 'what works' in dropout prevention and recovery" (p. 23).

Table 4
State Funding of At-Risk Programs

State	FUNDING			METHOD	
	No Specific At-Risk Funding	Funding for Selected Groups	At-Risk Funding	Competitive Grants	Formula-Based Funding
Alabama	●				
Alaska	●	●		●	
Arizona			●	●	
Arkansas	●				
California		●	●	●	●
Colorado			●	●	
Connecticut			●		●
Delaware			●	●	
Florida	●	●			●
Georgia	●	●			●
Hawaii	●	●			●
Idaho	●	●			●
Illinois	●	●		●	
Indiana			●	●	
Iowa			●	●	●
Kansas			●	●	
Kentucky	●	●		●	
Louisiana	●				
Maine	●				
Maryland	●	●		●	
Massachusetts	●	●		●	
Michigan	●	●			●
Minnesota	●	●			●
Mississippi	●	●			●
Missouri	●				
Montana	●				
Nebraska	●				
Nevada	●				
New Hampshire	●				
New Jersey	●	●			●
New Mexico			●	●	●
New York			●	●	●
North Carolina			●		●
North Dakota	●				●
Ohio	●	●			●
Oklahoma			●	●	
Oregon	●			●	●
Pennsylvania	●	●		●	
Rhode Island			●		●
South Carolina	●	●			●
South Dakota			●	●	●
Tennessee	●	●			●
Texas			●		●
Utah			●		●
Vermont	●	●			●
Virginia	●	●			●
Washington	●				
West Virginia	●	●			
Wisconsin			●		●
Wyoming	●	●			

State recognition of at-risk youth in funding formulas has been very limited. In a national survey, McDonough (1990) found that only 21 states had an official definition of at-risk youth. In several states, the focus was more on high school-age youth who were potential dropouts than on children in the primary grades. Several states have been selected as examples of efforts being made to address the specific needs of at-risk children in the early grades. In the following discussion, examples of state programs have been grouped into those that fund programs targeted on grades K–3, fund all grade levels, and recognize at-riskness, but provide no funds.

FUNDED PROGRAMS FOR GRADES K-3

Only a few states are funding programs specifically designed for at-risk children in grades K–3.

Arizona

Arizona has a discretionary grant program for at-risk children in grades K–3. A separate smaller discretionary grant program is targeted to secondary level at-risk pupils and dropout prevention programs. At-risk children are defined as those students who have dropped out or who have identifiable characteristics, including academic and economic factors, that are recognized as increasing the likelihood of their dropping out of the educational system.

Colorado

Colorado has a discretionary grant program targeted for the development of preschool services for four-and five-year-old children who are in need of language development. Colorado has no official definition for at-risk youth; however, the state has identified a series of factors which increase a youth's at-riskness.

FUNDED PROGRAMS FOR ALL GRADE LEVELS

Connecticut

Connecticut provides funds for at-risk youth through the state funding formula by a weighted pupil count. Additionally, the state employs an index of need to target funds to districts with a high percentage of at-risk youth. Need is determined by the number of students in a district who score at or below the remediation level on state achievement tests. The state also funds some

33

programming through categorical grants. Connecticut defines youth at risk as those who are in danger of academic failure or dropping out of school.

Delaware

Delaware has no official definition for at-risk youth, but the state does provide funding through state competitive discretionary grants matched by local school district resources. Within a particular legislated program titled "Children-at-Risk Intervention Program," at-risk youth are defined as "those children who exhibit or who can be reasonably projected to exhibit poor performance in traditional academic programs and classroom settings and are, therefore, considered to have an increased propensity toward dropping out of school or who upon graduation are likely to enter society without the skills necessary to be responsible individuals, competent employees, or successful continuing education students."

Georgia

Georgia does not specifically fund at-risk programs. Through categorical grants, the state funds a number of special instruction assistance programs that target segments of the at-risk youth population. The state definition defines at-risk children at three educational levels: preschool, primary grades, and intermediate-secondary grades. Among the characteristics cited that place a child at risk are living in poverty, limited English proficiency, poor academic performance, retention in one or more grades, frequent absences, emotional problems, health problems, behavior problems, student's use of alcohol or drugs, pregnancy or parenthood, and attempted suicide.

Indiana

Indiana provides funds through competitive discretionary grants. The state has no official definition for at-risk youth, but the state department of education has guidelines for local units to develop programs. Within the guidelines is a list of indicators of risk that include low academic achievement, low self-esteem, under-developed language skills, discipline problems, delinquent and/or disruptive behavior, poor attitude toward school and teachers, and poor school attendance. Since 1984, Indiana's "Prime Time" program has allocated state funds to reduce class size in the primary grades.

New Mexico

New Mexico provides funds for at-risk programming through its general equalized aid formula and also allocates funds through competitive grants. The state department of education defines at-risk students as those whose school achievement, progress toward graduation, and/or preparation for employment are in serious jeopardy.

Ohio

Ohio funds programs that target segments of the at-risk population through categorical grants. The state also has established grants for research and development of at-risk and excellence programs. The state has no official definition for at-risk youth; however, the Ohio Department of Education defines at-risk children and youth as individuals from birth through 21 years of age who are unlikely to complete elementary and secondary school successfully and to acquire the skills necessary for higher education and/or employment. The department also lists contributing factors of at-riskness that include alcohol/drug abuse, cyclical poverty, delinquency/truancy, family abuse/neglect, health condition, inadequate readiness skills/developmental delay, inappropriate school curriculum, inappropriate school placement, limited English/non-English speaking, low self-esteem, and pregnancy/parenting.

Oklahoma

Oklahoma allocates funds for at-risk programming on an annual basis through two competitive grant programs. At-risk youth are members of a household or family whose income is at or below the poverty level under criteria used by the U.S. Bureau of the Census; or they have not made substantial progress in mastering skills that are appropriate for students of their age; or they have grades that consistently indicate major underachievement; or they have been retained in a grade for one or more years; or they have been a school dropout or have had excessive absences during a school year; or they have been determined to be at risk based on assessment by school staff familiar with the students' health, social, or family status. Influences may include, but are not limited to, evidence of abuse of the students, the students' use of alcohol or drugs, pregnancy or parenthood, delinquent behavior, or attempted suicide.

South Carolina

South Carolina uses categorical grants to fund a wide range of district programs that include parenting programs, mentoring programs, summer enrichment, summer employment, and individual remediation. Projects are funded for three years. However, the state has no official definition for at-risk youth.

South Dakota

South Dakota has established an at-risk trust fund with the interest to be used for at-risk programming; the funds will be distributed to local school districts through competitive discretionary grants. An at-risk youth is any person under the age of 21 who is in danger of not graduating from high school or of not attaining personal, economic, and social sufficiency.

Texas

Texas provides at-risk program funds under the state compensatory education program, which is a weighted allocation based on a district's free/reduced-price lunch population. A person below 21 years of age who meets one or more of the following criteria is identified as at risk: (1) has not been promoted one or more times in grades 1–6 and continues to be unable to master the essential elements in the 7th or higher grade level; (2) is two or more years below grade level in reading or mathematics; (3) has failed at least two courses in one or more semesters and is not expected to graduate within four years of the time the student entered the 9th grade; or (4) has failed one or more of the reading, writing, or mathematics sections of the most recent statewide achievement test beginning with the 7th grade.

Utah

Utah provides at-risk programming by a combination of a base grant per school district and a formula allocation to school districts based upon the incidence of at-risk youth within the district. A student at risk is any student who, because of his/her individual needs, requires some kind of uniquely designed intervention in order to achieve literacy, graduate, and be prepared for transition from school to postschool options. Without appropriate intervention, a student is at increased risk for failing to achieve commensurate with his/her ability, for truancy, and for dropping out. Without appropriate intervention, such a student may not be able to participate meaningfully in society as a competent, productive, caring, and responsible citizen.

RECOGNITION OF THE PROBLEM WITHOUT FUNDING

Alaska

Alaska does not provide specific funding for programs and services for at-risk youth, but has adopted a broad definition: "At-risk students are those who are not acquiring the knowledge, skills and attitudes necessary for success in their next level of schooling, skills which will enable responsible citizenship, and/or productivity and personal fulfillment." Even though the state does not specifically fund at-risk programming, it does fund programs that are targeted at students who would be considered at risk. Examples include suicide prevention project, summer school, life skills curriculum, and a talent bank.

Arkansas

Arkansas does not provide specific funding for at-risk programs, but the state has adopted a definition. At-risk children are those enrolled in school or eligible for enrollment, whose progress toward graduation, school achievement, or preparation for employment and futures as productive workers and citizens who are jeopardized by a variety of health, social, educational, familial, and economic factors. They are the children with special needs who are underserved, categorized, ignored, and unchallenged and for whom expectations are low.

Oregon

Oregon does not provide funds specifically for at-risk programming and has no official definition for at-risk youth. The state funds a student retention initiative, and a special grant program for promoting at-risk programs is funded through the governor's office. For several years, the state has provided school districts with initial funding for a child development specialist, but the funding is reduced from an initial $10,000 to $1,000 after the fourth year (Peck 1989).

Washington

Washington does not provide funds for at-risk programming, but at-risk students are defined as those in elementary, middle, or secondary school who are identified as not succeeding in school, have considered dropping out of school, or have dropped out of school.

Wyoming

Wyoming does not specifically fund at-risk programs but does fund a state compensatory education program. At-risk youth are defined as individuals of school age who appear likely to fail because of economical, social, and academic conditions.

Table 5
Summary Evaluation of Funding Alternatives*

EVALUATION CRITERIA	COMPETITIVE DISCRETIONARY GRANTS	UNIT ALLOCATIONS	EXCESS COST REIMBURSEMENTS	CATEGORICAL GRANTS	INDEX OF NEED	EQUALIZED PER PUPIL ALLOCATIONS
STABILITY AND PREDICTABILITY	(−) • Pilot/demonstration projects • Specified time period • May not be renewed	(+) • Funds awarded based on qualified number of units	(+) • Funds reimbursed for extra cost of providing special service	(+) • Funds allocated based on number of students identified for services	(+) • Funds allocated based on indicators of student need	(+) • Funds allocated based on number of students identified for services
ADEQUACY	(−) • Funding narrowly targeted • Unserved and underserved target population	(±) • Adequate if funding level sufficient • Adequate if full reimbursement • Percentage reimbursement may penalize poorer districts	(±) • Adequate if funding level sufficient • Adequate if full reimbursement • Percentage reimbursement may penalize poorer districts	(+) • Adequate if funding level sufficient	(±) • Adequate if funding level sufficient • Adequate if adjusted so all districts quality	(+) • Adequate if funding level sufficient
EFFICIENCY	(+) • Pre-planned, specified program • Anticipated cost/ budget	(−) • Encourages traditional delivery modes • May encourage greater use of specialized personnel • Disincentive to mainstream • Can encourage minimum class size • Minimal data burden	(−) • Full reimbursement provides incentive to maximize costs • Percentage reimbursement may offer incentive for prudent use of funds • Detailed cost accounting required	(±) • Targeted use of funds • Programs may be based on available dollars rather than educational need • Incentive for labeling children • May encourage placement in higher reimbursement programs • Detailed cost accounting not required	(+) • Provides resources based on single measure • Incentive for mainstreaming • Minimal data burden	(±) • Targeted use of funds • Programs may be based on available dollars rather than educational need • Incentive for labeling children • May encourage placement in higher reimbursement programs • Detailed cost accounting not required • Requires some district participation

*Ordered from least to most preferred, according to McDonough's (1990) survey.

Table 5 (Continued)

EVALUATION CRITERIA	COMPETITIVE DISCRETIONARY GRANTS	UNIT ALLOCATIONS	EXCESS COST REIMBURSEMENTS	CATEGORICAL GRANTS	INDEX OF NEED	EQUALIZED PER PUPIL ALLOCATIONS
ACCOUNTA-BILITY	+ • Highly accountable • Program evaluation component • Pre-specified budget progress updates	+ • Able to track targeted use of funds to units	+ • High degree of accountability • Detailed cost accounting required • Direct connection between funding and expenditures	+ • Funds based on identified number of children • Not as easy to track targeted use of funds	− • Least ability to track monies to targeted population	+ • Funds based on identified number of children • Not as easy to track targeted use of funds
EQUITY (TAXPAYER)	− • Not equalized	± • Equitable if equalized	− • Not equalized • Benefits wealthier, suburban, unified districts	− • Not equalized	+ • Benefits poorer, smaller, urban, rural districts	+ • Equalized
EQUITY (STUDENT)	− • Limited target population • May not reflect distribution of problem	± • May penalize smaller districts due to lack of minimum number to qualify for unit	+ • Equitable if total cost reimbursed; If not, may penalize smaller districts	+ • Provides fixed amount per identified student	+ • Monies targeted based on magnitude of the problem	− • May penalize smaller districts • May penalize high wealth/high need districts
RESPON-SIVENESS	− • Possible only partial funds awarded • Not responsive to total state need	− • Limited flexibility • Disincentive for innovation	+ • Allows program flexibility to meet student needs • Allows updating of funding amounts as program changes occur	+ • Allows for program flexibility to meet student needs	+ • Highly flexible • Incentive for innovation	+ • Allows for program flexibility to meet student needs
NON-MANIPULA-BILITY	+ • Highly non-manipulable • Terms pre-specified	± • Less direct incentive to over-classify	± • Manipulable in terms of providing program and cost data • Disincentive for overclassifying	± • Basically non-manipulable • Incentive to overclassify	+ • Non-manipulable to degree that funding is based on socio-economic factors outside district control	± • Basically non-manipulable • Incentive to overclassify
TOTAL SCORE	+ = 3 ± = 0 − = 4	+ = 2 ± = 3 − = 2	+ = 3 ± = 3 − = 1	+ = 4 ± = 3 − = 0	+ = 5 ± = 1 − = 1	+ = 4 ± = 3 − = 0

Chapter 6

FUNDING STRATEGIES

HOW SHOULD PROGRAMS BE FUNDED?

Alternatives for states to use in providing funds for at-risk programs can be grouped into six groups based on (a) their frequency of use in need-based funding mechanisms, and/or (b) their being preferred by state and national experts on at-risk programming and school finance (Hartman 1980; McDonough 1990). Among the most widely used strategies to adjust state allocations based on differentiated need are pupil weights, categorical aid, discretionary grants, excess cost reimbursements, and unit cost allocations (Webb, McCarthy, and Thomas 1988). A more recent addition is the index of need used in Arizona and Connecticut (Arizona Department of Education 1989, State of Connecticut Department of Education 1989).

FUNDING OPTIONS

In a national survey McDonough (1990) found that 52 percent of the respondents ranked pupil weights as their first or second choice. The next most preferred option was categorial aid (46%). Index of need was preferred by 44 percent of the respondents. Less preferred options were excess cost reimbursements (30%), competitive discretionary grants (19%), and unit cost allocations (14%). Each of these alternative funding strategies is described in the following discussions.

Pupil Weights

The theoretical basis for pupil weights is that different dollar amounts per pupil are needed to provide programs and services to overcome the variation in the educational needs of students (Webb, McCarthy, and Thomas 1988). Typically, a weight of 1.00 is assigned to elementary school children in the intermediate grades who are not in special programs; other weights are assigned based on the comparative costs of educating a student enrolled in other grade levels or in specialized programs.

Categorical Aid

A common method in many states for allocating resources to special-need students is through categorical grants that are used in addition to the basic state allocations. Categorical grants may be distributed based on a per-pupil amount, per-classroom unit, or per school or school district with special demographic characteristics. The grants may be straight sum amounts based on a fixed amount of money per child, or they may be a percentage of approved costs for educating a specific category of child (Hartman 1980).

Competitive Discretionary Grants

Under this alternative, school districts compete for funds by submitting a project proposal and an application of need along with assurances of compliance with state laws and regulations relative to the grant. Assurances might include documentation of the target group to be served and a statement that grant monies would be utilized to supplement and not supplant current district programs. The application is reviewed on its merits by the funding agency, and awards are made to the school districts whose applications best meet the criteria for funding (Sherman 1987).

Excess Cost Reimbursements

In some states, the excess costs model is used to provide state aid to high-cost programs. In this model, the difference between the cost of educating a regular elementary school student and a student enrolled in a special program is the excess cost. A state may pay all of the excess cost of a program, or a percentage of the excess cost. Cost-based formulas require detailed cost-accounting procedures, since actual program expenditures are reimbursed (Hartman 1980).

Unit Cost Allocations

This funding strategy allocates resources based on the number of teachers or classroom units needed for specific programs, rather than on the number of students in a program (Webb, McCarthy, and Thomas 1988). Under this resource-based adjustment, a minimum number of children with special needs qualifies a district to receive full funding for a classroom or teacher. State standards are usually established regarding minimum and maximum class size (Hartman 1980).

Index of Need

In this allocation strategy, individual students are not identified for funding calculations. The index is a proxy for the magnitude of need in a given district, rather than being a predictor of the number of students, or a count or listing of actual students. Quantifiable indicators are selected to provide a composite view of the relative magnitude of the need. Limiting factors of an index of need using multiple indicators include the assumption that all indicators are of equal importance, and that valid and reliable data are available.

RANK OF THE FUNDING OPTIONS

By using a systematic evaluation, the relative merits of each funding option can be analyzed. The design of the following analysis involved two steps. The first was a review of need-based funding methods used to date and an analysis of potential incentives and disincentives associated with these methods. The second was a review of existing evaluation criteria that could be used to evaluate funding alternatives to provide fiscal resources for programs and services for at-risk youth.

INCENTIVES AND DISINCENTIVES OF NEED-BASED FUNDING ALTERNATIVES

The issues become the way in which different funding alternatives affect the distribution of monies, and how the inherent incentives and disincentives of each funding alternative affect program and management issues. Hartman (1980) analyzed those issues relevant to need-based formulas that were utilized to fund special education programs. His analysis is also useful in evaluating options for at-risk funding; decision makers can learn from the incentives and disincentives that resulted from various funding mechanisms used in allocating monies for special education.

In reviewing each of the need-based formulas, Hartman addressed several program and management issues. He categorized special education funding strategies into three broad types: resource-based formulas (unit allocation), child-based formulas (categorical grants and equalized per-pupil weights), and cost-based formulas (percentage and excess cost reimbursements).

Resource-Based Formulas

The resource-based formulas offer a reduced incentive to over classify students, since funding is based on allocated teacher/classroom units rather directly related to each child in the program. A child's disability is determined through eligibility standards, while funding is based on a range in the number of eligible students used to allocate each unit of service or number of personnel. These formulas, however, discourage mainstreaming, since funding is based on the number of students used to justify a unit or teacher of a special class.

Child-Based Formulas

The child-based formulas are the most likely to encourage overclassification of children. They provide the greatest incentive to serve unserved populations, but also have provided the strongest incentives for maximizing class size and for labeling children as handicapped. Child-based formulas provide some funding to all districts, but pose a problem for smaller districts with low numbers of qualifying children. The number of children may not generate

43

enough monies to fund a complete program. Planning under these formulas is less straightforward, and there may be a tendency to base programs on available dollars rather than on student needs. One advantage of the child-based approach is that school districts can explore the possibility of innovative delivery systems. As with the other formulas, funding cannot be tracked to expenditures on a specific child. Expenditures are accounted for and reported on an aggregated basis for each program or classroom unit. Changes are difficult to document or explain, because they are reported in program or classroom unit cost terms, then recalculated into per-pupil expenditures.

Cost-Based Formulas

Cost-based formulas offer the least incentive for overclassification. Percentage costs require districts to pay a portion of the increased costs, and excess cost formulas are theoretically fiscally neutral if all costs are reimbursed. Cost-based formulas require more detailed accounting records than the other types of formulas, since the expenditures themselves are reimbursed. For tracking the use of funds, the cost-based formulas are most effective, since reimbursement amounts are the actual expenditures. They also accommodate future increased program costs if funded on the basis of actual costs incurred.

As illustrated by the previous discussion, Hartman's (1980) analysis of need-based funding formulas provides a framework for decision making. It allows policymakers to (a) select a funding approach and (b) consider rules and regulations that could mitigate the problem areas of that approach so that the resulting funding mechanism would maximize the impact of programs to serve at-risk youth.

CRITERIA FOR EVALUATING PROGRAMS

From the school finance research literature, Jordan (1989) has identified a set of criteria that could be used in evaluating alternative methods for allocating state funds to programs for at-risk youth.

1. *Stability and Predictability.* If programs to serve at-risk students are to continue without adversely affecting school district tax rates, state funds should not fluctuate from one year to the next. Initial funding for a program carries an implied commitment to continue funding until sufficient evidence is available to determine whether the program is a success or whether the need for funding continues.

2. *Adequacy.* The level of funding should be sufficient to enable the local school districts to provide the needed services and programs. Unrealistic expectations and an insufficient level of

funds are legitimate concerns when the state decides to provide funds for a specific program or target group of students, or to require that districts provide a special program to serve a particular group of students. Local school administrators are very sensitive to the nagging issue of "unfunded" or "underfunded" mandates.

3. *Efficiency.* In this context, efficiency refers to components in the funding formula that encourage cost containment, targeted use of funds, program selection based on maximization of resources, minimal data burden on local districts, and mainstreaming of at-risk students into the regular school program.

4. *Accountability.* Accountability refers to the extent to which special funding for at-risk students is expended for programs or services to serve the target group that generated the funds rather than their being diverted to programs or services for other students or diluted because of the absence of a discrete program to serve the target students.

5. *Equity.* Equity can be viewed in two dimensions—student equity and taxpayer equity. Student equity is attained when a district's entitlement under the state school finance program is based on the different levels of funding required to provide individual students with an educational program congruent with their particular needs. Taxpayer equity is attained when the state school finance program provides equal revenues (combined from state and local tax sources) for equal units of tax effort. If all funds are allocated to a few districts whose students have special characteristics but not greater need, then the student equity criterion will not be satisfied. If the differences in the fiscal capacity of school districts are not considered in the allocation of state funds, then the taxpayer equity criterion will not be satisfied.

6. *Responsiveness.* Districts and pupils differ from a variety of perspectives. One cannot assume that all students projected to be at risk have the same types of needs, so a state funding program should be sufficiently flexible to accommodate different types of programs as well as students with different programmatic needs. Among localities, the extent of out-of-school services will vary among school districts, and some districts will have to provide services that are available from other agencies in other districts.

7. *Non-Manipulability.* Especially with a new program, student counts and program definitions should be sufficiently precise and

objective to ensure that local school officials cannot manipulate the student counts and program data to benefit their district in an unfair manner.

EVALUATION OF THE OPTIONS

Lyons (1990a) evaluated the efficacy of each of the previously described funding alternatives using Jordan's (1989) seven evaluation criteria discussed above. In addition, she incorporated Hartman's (1980) incentives and disincentives of alternative need-based funding options where applicable. The Hartman components included incentives and disincentives for classification and assignment of students, flexibility in program delivery systems, program and fiscal planning, and cost reporting and containment.

As shown in Table 5, among the alternatives, discretionary grants scored lowest. This option met three of the seven criteria: efficiency, accountability, and non-manipulability. The three top-rated alternatives were an index of need, the equalized per-pupil allocation, and the per-pupil categorical grant.

The equalized per-pupil and the per-pupil categorical grant each scored positively on four criteria: stability and predictability, adequacy, accountability, and responsiveness. These alternatives offered great flexibility and the capacity for multiple options through state incentives and mandates. The major drawbacks are that they necessitate the labeling of children to receive services, and that they may put a greater fiscal burden on those districts that have the greatest number of at-risk youth to serve.

The index of need scored highest of the six alternative funding strategies. It scored positively on five of the criteria: stability and predictability, efficiency, equity, responsiveness, and non-manipulability. For the adequacy criterion, it has the potential for providing adequate services if it is adjusted so that all districts are eligible to qualify for some level of funding. The advantages of the index of need are that students do not have to be labeled to receive services, it allows for maximum flexibility in programming, and it has the potential for maximizing educational equity. Its primary disadvantage is the lack of accountability inherent in the funding mechanism. If an index of need were selected as the funding alternative, policymakers would want to build accountability measures into the rules and regulations.

In a simulation study of alternative funding methods for at-risk youth conducted on a prototype state, Lyons (1990a) found that the three top-rated alternatives tended to benefit different types of school districts. The index of need alternative tended to benefit poor districts; urban, rural, and independent area districts; and districts with small populations. The categorical grants tended to benefit wealthy, suburban, and unified school districts. Equalized per-pupil allocations tended to benefit large, moderately wealthy, suburban, and unified districts.

Chapter 7

CONCLUSION

THE MAJOR POLICY ISSUES

Accepting the underlying assumption that the at-risk dilemma can best be resolved by the state's facilitating dynamic, innovative approaches to programming, several possible policy directions were identified that would maximize local innovation and decision making. Based on an analysis of the general condition of programs and services for at-risk youth, the following public policy choices are among those that should be considered by state-level policymakers as they authorize and fund programs for at-risk youth.

Who Should Be in the Target Group?

Defining the target group for at-risk programs is difficult because of the lack of agreement on a definition of at-risk youth. Among the contributing factors are the variations in conditions among schools and school districts that result in a child being considered to be at risk. Another decision point in identification of the target group for at-risk programs is whether to serve all students who are potentially at risk or to limit the programs to students at certain age/grade levels.

One policy consideration is the extent to which local school districts should be permitted to develop criteria for identifying students as being at risk. Another policy consideration is that criteria for the identification of students and the allocation of funds based on target group/program criteria should not provide an incentive for the district to classify students into programs so that the district receives more state funds.

Target group decisions can be made at different levels. National criteria can be adapted to local conditions, and identification criteria such as those discussed previously might be considered. At least two options can be used to identify the target group. First, the state legislature or state board of education can adopt a top-down stance and impose target group criteria upon local school districts. Second, given the diversity of conditions associated with a student being at risk, responsibility for identifying students to be served can be delegated to the local school district.

How Should Programs Be Delivered?

The most prevalent programs have an academic focus and are delivered either in a class or small group. Research about "what works" in programs for at-risk youth is limited; therefore, state program restrictions and prescriptions may not be advisable because of the lack of an information/research base about effective and ineffective programs for at-risk youth. Even with the lack of a strong research base, there does appear to be some consensus that pullout programs may be detrimental because they tend to disrupt the basic instructional program of the students who are "pulled out" (Coley and Goertz 1987).

Should Funds Be Traced to the Target Population?

Under all funding alternatives except the at-risk index, funding could follow the student if the rules and regulations indicate that funds are to be expended on the student who generated the funds. One of the dilemmas with strict adherence to the principle of the funds following the child is that funding levels for programs may be insufficient in some instances and more than sufficient in others; consequently, there would appear to be some merit in providing school districts with a degree of flexibility in the use of funds.

What Program Participation Standards Should Be Used?

In any program with multiple delivery components, the question may be raised about the number of programs in which a student may be participating. In some programs, pupil counting problems are of less concern, but multiple focus programs provide local school officials with double or multiple student counting opportunities. An additional concern is related to the possibility that a student identified as "at risk" could become a source of special income for the school district. When this occurs, the school district may be reluctant to indicate that the student no longer is "at risk."

What Outcome Measures Should Be Used?

Various outcome measures may be used; they range from reductions in the dropout rate and discipline referrals to increased attendance and improved performance on standardized tests. However, given the current status of programs for these youth, the best outcome measures may be observable changes in the student/school factors that were used in designing programs and identifying program participants. Pre- and postprogram data will provide information concerning changes that have taken place during the course of the program.

WHAT NEEDS TO BE DONE?

The merits of different policy choices should be weighed as decisions are made about program design and implementation. One policy choice is whether or not the best way to address the at-risk dilemma is to encourage local creativity, diversity, and flexibility in designing and delivering programs. Other choices are related to the target group and the focus of programs. The research reported in this publication points to several possible policy directions leading to the selection of a funding alternative that would maximize local innovation and decision making.

First, programs for at-risk youth are in an evolutionary stage. In view of the dearth of program evaluation data and cost-effectiveness studies and the variations in target groups and programs, selection of one of the traditional school finance formulas to fund at-risk programs may be premature.

Second, immediate state action to provide funding for programs to service at-risk youth is imperative because the social and economic cost of delay is too great.

Third, if the goal is to ensure that all eligible students receive adequate services, using a fiscally equalized funding approach may be counterproductive. Equalized options may penalize property-wealthy inner-city districts that often have the highest incidence of at-risk youth.

Fourth, if the public policy goal is to target resources on those districts with the greatest need and to encourage local creativity in addressing the problem, the index of need appears to be the preferred funding alternative.

One of the conceptual challenges in the use of the index of need is selection of the variables to be used in developing the index. There is probably no single best set of indicators for all states. Each state would need to identify the set of indicators that best reflects the state's need and its unique set of circumstances.

REFERENCES

Arizona Department of Education. *The At-Risk Status of Arizona School Districts*. Ed. STAT Report. Phoenix, Ariz.: Arizona Department of Education, 1989.

Brodinsky, B. *Students at Risk: Problems and Solutions*. Arlington, Va.: American Association of School Administrators Critical Issues Report, 1989.

Brown, B. "Head Start: How Research Changed Public Policy." *Young Children* 40, no. 5 (1985):9–14.

Butler, O. "Early Help for Kids At Risk: Our Nation's Next Investment." *Preventive Attention* (January 1989) Washington, D.C.: National Education Association, 1989.

Chambers, J. G. "Cost and Price Level Adjustments to State Aid for Education: A Theoretical and Empirical Review in Educational Need and Fiscal Capacity." In *Perspectives in State School Support Programs*, edited by K. F. Jordan and N. Cambron-McCabe, 39–86. Second Annual Yearbook of the American Education Finance Association. Cambridge, Mass.: Ballinger Publishing, 1981.

Charlesworth, R. " 'Behind' Before They Start?" *Young Children* (March 1989): 5–13.

Clifford, J. C. "A Taxonomy of Dropout Prevention Strategies in Selected School Districts." University Microfilms International No. 8710125. Ph.D. diss., Columbia University, New York, 1987.

Coley, R. J., and Goertz, M.E. *Children at Risk*. Council of Chief State School Officers, Washington, D.C., 1987.

Committee for Economic Development. *Investing in Our Children: Business and the Public Schools*. CED Report, 47–51. New York, 1987.

Cox, J. L. *Study of High School Dropouts in Appalachia*.Center for Educational Studies. RTI Report No. 234 U., 1985.

Curry, N. "Presentation to the Pennsylvania State Board of Education." *Young Children* 45, no. 3 (1990): 17–23.

Davis, W. E., and McCaul, E. J. *At-Risk Children and Youth: A Crisis in Our Schools and Society*. Orono, Maine: University of Maine, 1990.

Edelman, M. W. "Economic Issues Related to Child Care and Early Childhood Education." *Teachers College Record* 90, no. 3 (1989): 343–51.

Fine, M. "Why Adolescents Drop Into and Out of Public High School." In *School Dropouts: Patterns and Policies*, 2d ed., edited by G. Natriello, 89–105). New York: Teachers College Press, 1987.

Foulks, B., and Morrow, R.D. "Academic Survival Skills for the Young Child at Risk for School Failure." *Journal of Educational Research* 82, no. 3 (1989):158–65.

Gersten, R.; Darch, C.; and Gleason, M. "Effectiveness of Direct Instruction Academic Kindergarten for Low-Income Students." *The Elementary School Journal* 89, no. 2 (1988): 227–40.

Goldring, E. B., and Presbrey, L.S. "Evaluation Preschool Programs: A Meta-Analytic Approach." *Educational Evaluation and Policy Analysis* 8 (1986): 179–88.

Government Accounting Office. *School Dropouts: Survey of Local Programs.* Report. GAO/HDR-87-108. Washington, D.C.: Government Printing Office, 1987.

Grossnickle, D. R. *High School Dropouts: Causes, Consequences and Cure.* Bloomington, Ind.: Phi Delta Kappa Educational Foundation, 1986.

Guidelines for the Priority School District Program. Hartford: State of Connecticut Department of Education, 1989. *Guidelines for the Priority School District Program.* Hartford: State of Connecticut Department of Education, 1989.

Hahn, A.; Danzberger, J.; and Lefkowitz, B. *Dropouts in America: Enough Is Known for Action: A Report for Policymakers and Grantsmakers.* Washington, D.C.: Institute for Educational Leadership, 1987.

Hansen, E. J. *Analysis of Principles and Issues: Rationale for Distributing Resources Unequally. In Financing, Organization and Governance of Education for Special Populations.* CERI/SF/80. Paris: Organization for Economic Cooperation and Development, 1980.

Hartman, W. T. "Policy Effects of Special Education Funding Formulas." *Journal of Education Finance* 6 (Fall 1988): 135–59.

Hebbeler, K. "An Old and a New Question on the Effects of Early Education for Children from Low-Income Families." *Educational Evaluation and Policy Analysis* 7: (1985): 207–16.

Hodge, M. V. "Improving Finance and Governance of Education for Special Populations." In *Perspectives in State School Support Programs*, edited by K. F. Jordan and N. Cambron-McCabe, 3–38. Second Annual Yearbook of the American Education Finance Association. Cambridge, Mass.: Ballinger Publishing, 1981.

Hodgkinson, H. *All One System: Demographics of Education, Kindergarten Through Graduate School.* Washington, D.C.: Institute for Educational Leadership, 1985.

Jordan K. F. "Introduction to School Finance." Tempe, Ariz.: College of Education, Arizona State University, 1989. Typescript.

Kunisawa, B. N. *A Nation in Crisis: The Dropout Dilemma.*, 61-65. Washington, D.C.: National Education Association, January, 1985.

Lennon, J. M. "The At-Risk Child: Early Identification, Intervention, and Evaluation of Early Childhood Strategies." Exit Project, Indiana University at South Bend, 1989. ERIC Document Reproduction Service. ED 310 860.

Levin, H. M. "Financing the Education of At-Risk Students." *Education Evaluation and Policy Analysis* 11 (Spring 1989): 47–60.

Lyons, T. S. "Alternative State Funding Allocation Methods for Local School District Programs to Serve 'At-Risk' Students." Ph.D. diss., Arizona State University, Tempe, Arizona, 1990a.

———. "An Evaluation of Developmental and Transition Programs in the Peoria Unified School District." Research report. Peoria Unified School District, Peoria, Arizona, 1990b.

McDonough, J. T. "A Survey of Opinions and Attitudes Toward State At-Risk Program Focus, Delivery, and Funding." Ph.D. diss., Arizona State University, Tempe, Arizona, 1990.

Madden, N. A., and Slavin, R. E. *Effective Pull-Out Programs for Students At Risk* (Report No. 20). Baltimore, Md.: Johns Hopkins University, 1987.

Mann, D. "Can We Help Dropouts: Thinking About the Undoable." In *School Dropouts: Patterns and Policies.* 2d ed., edited by G. Natriello, 3-19. New York: Teachers College Press, 1987.

Morrison Institute for Public Policy. *The Arizona At-Risk Pilot Project: Serving Students in Grades K–3 and 7–12 Pursuant to HB 2217.* Tempe, Ariz.: Arizona State University, School of Public Affairs, 1988.

———.*1988–89 Status and Evaluation Report: The Arizona At-Risk Pilot Project: Serving Students in Grades K–3 and 7–12 Pursuant to HB 2217.* Tempe, Ariz.: School of Public Affairs, Arizona State University, November 1989.

National Governors' Association. *National Education Goals.* Washington, D.C.: Author, 1990.

Natriello, G.; Pallas, A. M.; and McDill, E. L. "Taking Stock: Renewing our Research Agenda on Causes and Consequences of Dropping Out." In *School Dropouts: Patterns and Policies* 2d ed., edited by G. Natriello, 168–178. New York: Teachers College Press, 1987.

Orr, M. T. *Keeping Students in School.* San Francisco: Jossey-Bass, 1987.

Peck, P. "The Child At Risk: In Search of Solutions." *Instructor* (January 1989): 29–30.

Peck, N.; Law, A.; and Mills, R. C. *Dropout Prevention: What We Have Learned.* Ann Arbor, Mich.: ERIC Counseling and Personnel Services Clearing House, 1987.

Ralph, J. "Improving Education for the Disadvantaged: Do We Know Whom to Help?" *Phi Delta Kappan* (January 1989): 395–401.